NATIONAL
GEOGRAPHIC
KiDS

Animal Kingdom

BOOK 8

D1431465

Tigers Have Stripes

ISBN 978-0-545-76650-0
10 9 8 7 6 5 4 3 2 1   14 15 16 17 18 19
Printed in China 145
First printing, September 2014

Photos © 2014: cover: subinpumsom/Thinkstock; 1: Denise Allison Coyle/Shutterstock, Inc.; 2: Sergey Uryadnikov/Shutterstock, Inc.;
3: Guan jiangchi/Shutterstock, Inc.; 4: Buquet Christophe/Shutterstock, Inc.; 5: Michael Mules/Alamy Images; 6: anat chant/
Shutterstock, Inc.; 7: LilKar/Shutterstock, Inc.; 8: Moments by Mullineux/Shutterstock, Inc.; 9: Geografika/Dreamstime;
10: The Washington Post/Getty Images; 11: Gerald Marella/Shutterstock, Inc.; 12: Dirk Ercken/Shutterstock, Inc.; 13: Piotr Naskrecki/
Getty Images; 14: anekoho/Shutterstock, Inc.; 15: Minden Pictures/Superstock, Inc.; 16 tiger: Denise Allison Coyle/Shutterstock, Inc.;
16 spider: Buquet Christophe/Shutterstock, Inc.; 16 bees: LilKar/Shutterstock, Inc.; 16 mouse: Moments by Mullineux/Shutterstock, Inc.;
16 woodpecker: Gerald Marella/Shutterstock, Inc.; 16 frog: Piotr Naskrecki/Getty Images; 16 zebras: anekoho/Shutterstock, Inc.

Scholastic Inc.

Bengal Tigers

Many **tigers** have **stripes**.

White Bengal Tiger

Some **tigers** are **white**.

Wasp Spider

Some **spiders** have **stripes**.

Translucent Spider

Other **spiders** are clear **like ice.**

Look at this **hive**!

Bumblebees

These bees all have **stripes**.

Field Mouse

Some **mice** have **stripes**.

This mouse has just one **line**.

Watch the woodpecker **glide**.

Striped Woodpecker

This bird has **stripes**.

Poison Dart Frog

This frog has **stripes**.

Tiger-Striped Lemur Frog

This frog has **stripes** on its **side**!

Zebra

All zebras have **stripes**.

Their **stripes** help them to **hide**.

Explore More Stripes Facts!

 The tiger is the largest wild cat in the world. It can weigh up to 720 pounds (363 kilograms) and stretch to about 6 feet (2 meters) long.

 The wasp spider builds its web in long grasses at dawn or dusk. It takes about an hour to complete the web.

 Bumblebees can fly at an altitude of 18,000 feet (5,500 meters), which is almost as high as Mount Kilimanjaro, the tallest mountain in Africa.

 Male mice sing songs with melodies and can be taught to vocalize different notes, just like humans, dolphins, and whales.

 Woodpeckers search for their favorite meal, carpenter ants, by digging large, rectangular holes in trees with their powerful beaks.

 The elaborate designs of a dart frog are deliberately bold to warn off potential predators.

 If a zebra is attacked, its family will come to its defense, circling the wounded zebra and attempting to drive away predators.